Learn About Horses

By Kathy Mann
Illustrated by Carol Berger

This book is for basic information purposes only and is no substitute for personal instruction from a qualified riding instructor. Horses are large, unpredictable, and potentially dangerous animals and it is strongly recommended that beginning riders seek guidance from a professional horse trainer or riding instructor whenever they are in contact with horses.

Published by Phelps L.L.C.
PO Box 174
Holt, MI 48842

www.phelpsllc.com

A horse is a large animal that people can ride.

Horses are herd animals. Herd animals like to live in groups and have friends. Horses have different sizes, colors, and personalities.

Some horses are tall and some horses are short. A smaller, shorter horse is a pony.

Horses have different shapes and sizes.
Some horses are big and wide.

Some horses are small and thin. A horse's different shapes and sizes make them better at different jobs.

People use a halter and a lead rope to lead the horse. The halter goes onto the horse's head and the lead rope snaps to the bottom halter ring near the horse's chin.

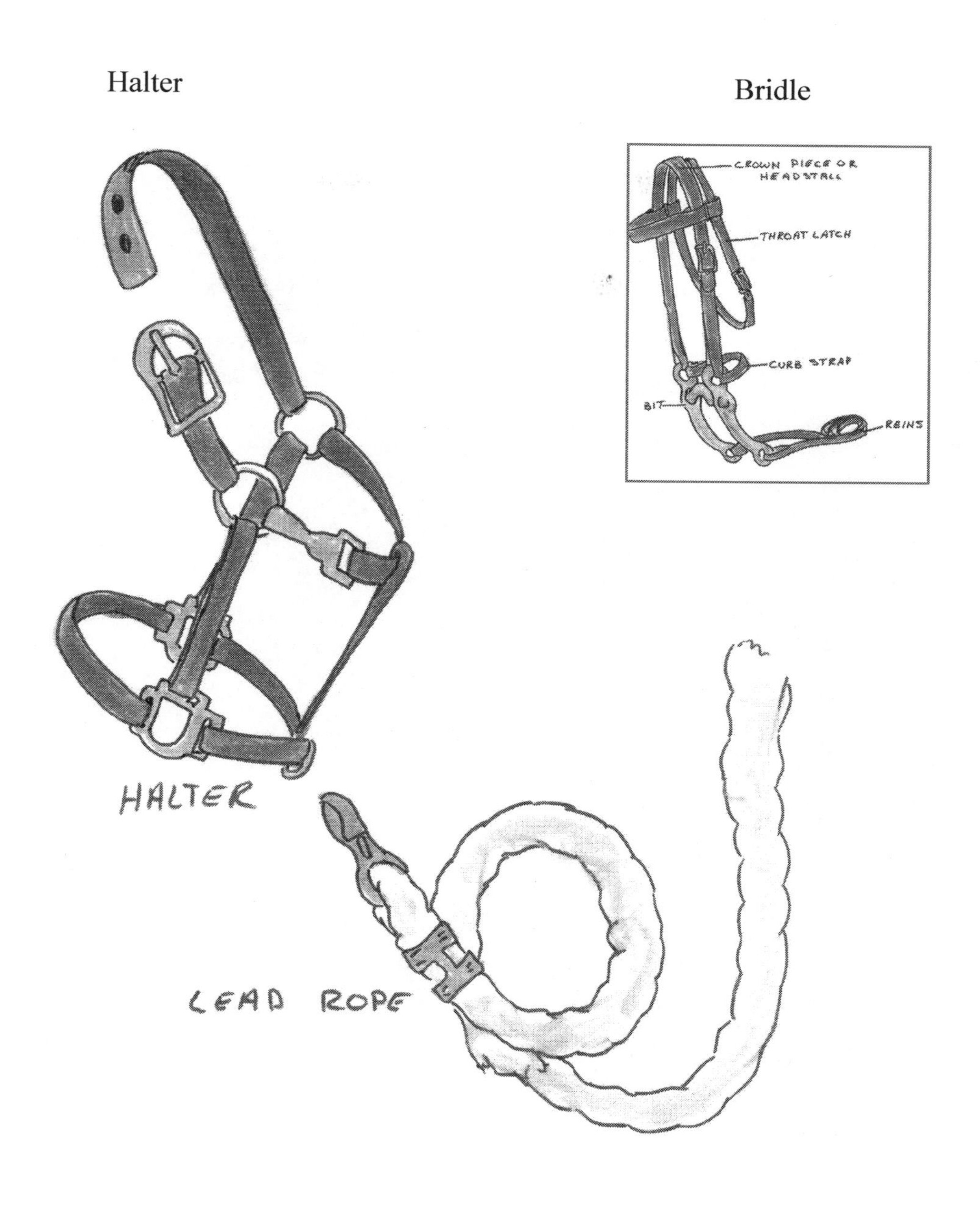

A halter does not have a bit.

A bit is the metal mouthpiece on a bridle and it goes into the horse's mouth.

Do not walk behind a horse because it may spook and kick you.

Horses do not see things that are behind them.

To catch a horse and halter it, walk toward it's neck and shoulder where it can see you.

The lead rope can be used around the horse's neck to hold the horse while you put the halter onto its head.

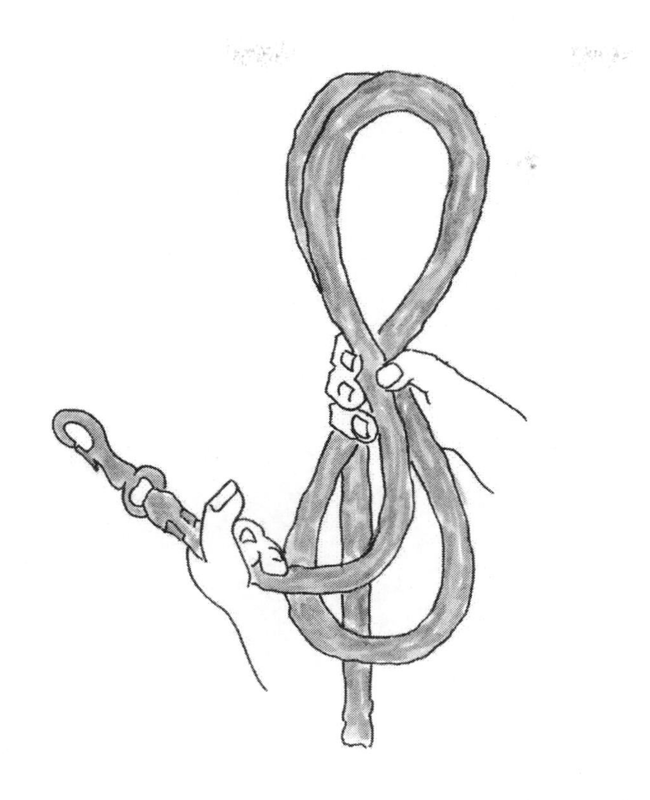

Hold the lead rope with your hand around the outside of the rope.

NEVER wrap the rope around your arm or hand. Never put your arm or hand inside the rope's loops becaue the horse could drag you if you get tangled in the rope.

You are the leader, but if you are too far back the horse could lead you.

Don't walk in front of the horse either,
or it could step on your heel.

Walk beside the horse's head to lead it.

Horses depend on people to take care of them and to keep them safe.

People take care of the horse's stall. A dirty stall has germs in it that can make a horse sick.

This stall has clean bedding and a happy and healthy horse. Bedding can be made from wood shavings (sawdust) or straw.

Fences keep horses in safe places where they won't be hit by cars or get hurt on things.

If a horse escapes, it could get hurt. People help keep horses safe by always closing and latching the gate.

Horses can get excited when they are set free and may kick out.

When you release a horse into a fence or stall, turn it around to face the gate or the door. Release the horse and then you step out.

Also, do not stand between the horse and a solid object, like a wall, because the horse could push you into the wall and you would not be able to escape.

When you release a horse, be ready to step out of its space.

Horses need a lot of clean and fresh water.

Horses eat grass or hay.

If a horse has trouble eating and is dropping its food, it may need to have its teeth floated. Floating is when the sharp edges are filed off.

A horse's teeth grow all the time and sometimes they grow sharp edges and the veterinarian or an equine dentist floats their teeth.

Horses also eat a few treats like apples, carrots and grain. But too many treats can make a horse sick.

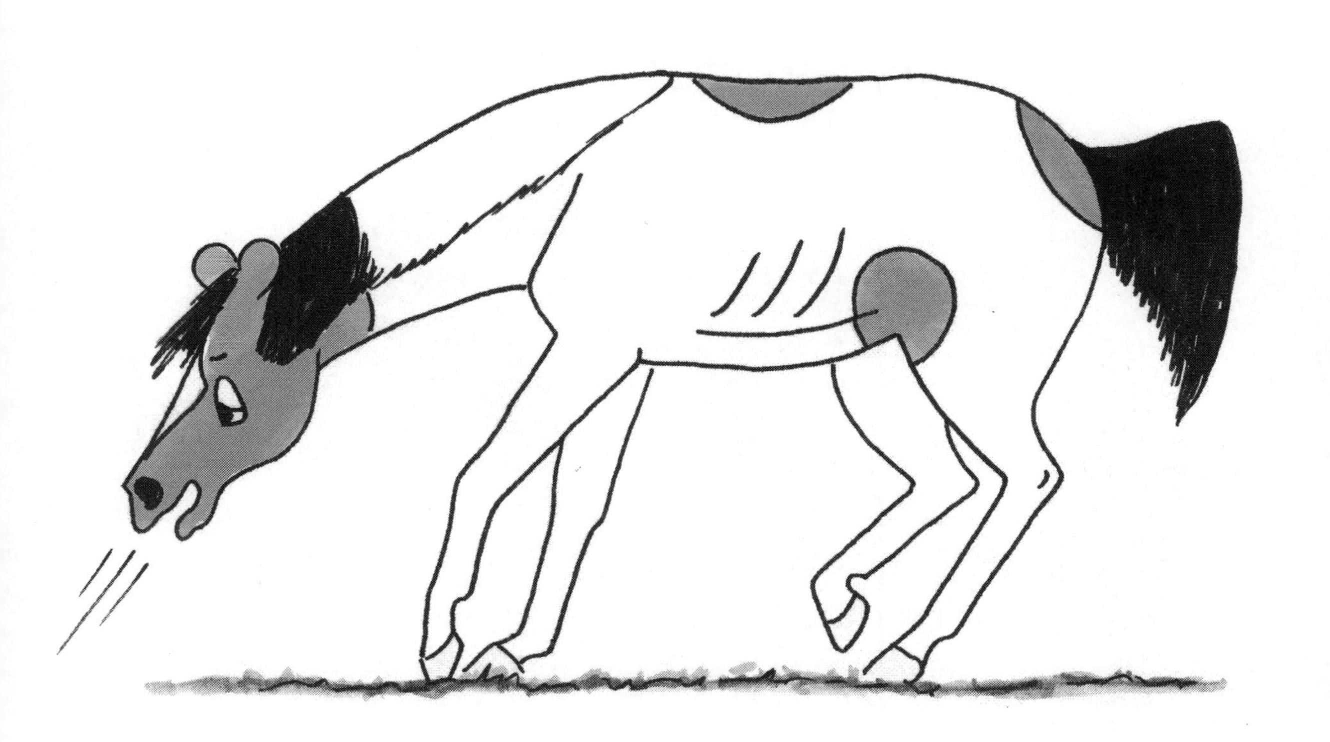

A horse may also get sick with a cold.

If a horse gets sick or hurt, the veterinarian will help him. A veterinarian is an animal doctor who has a lot of special medical training to help animals.

The veterinarian uses medicines and knowledge to help horses when they are sick or if there is an emergency and the horse is hurt.

The veterinarian also gives advice about what the horse should eat, its vaccinations, and care.

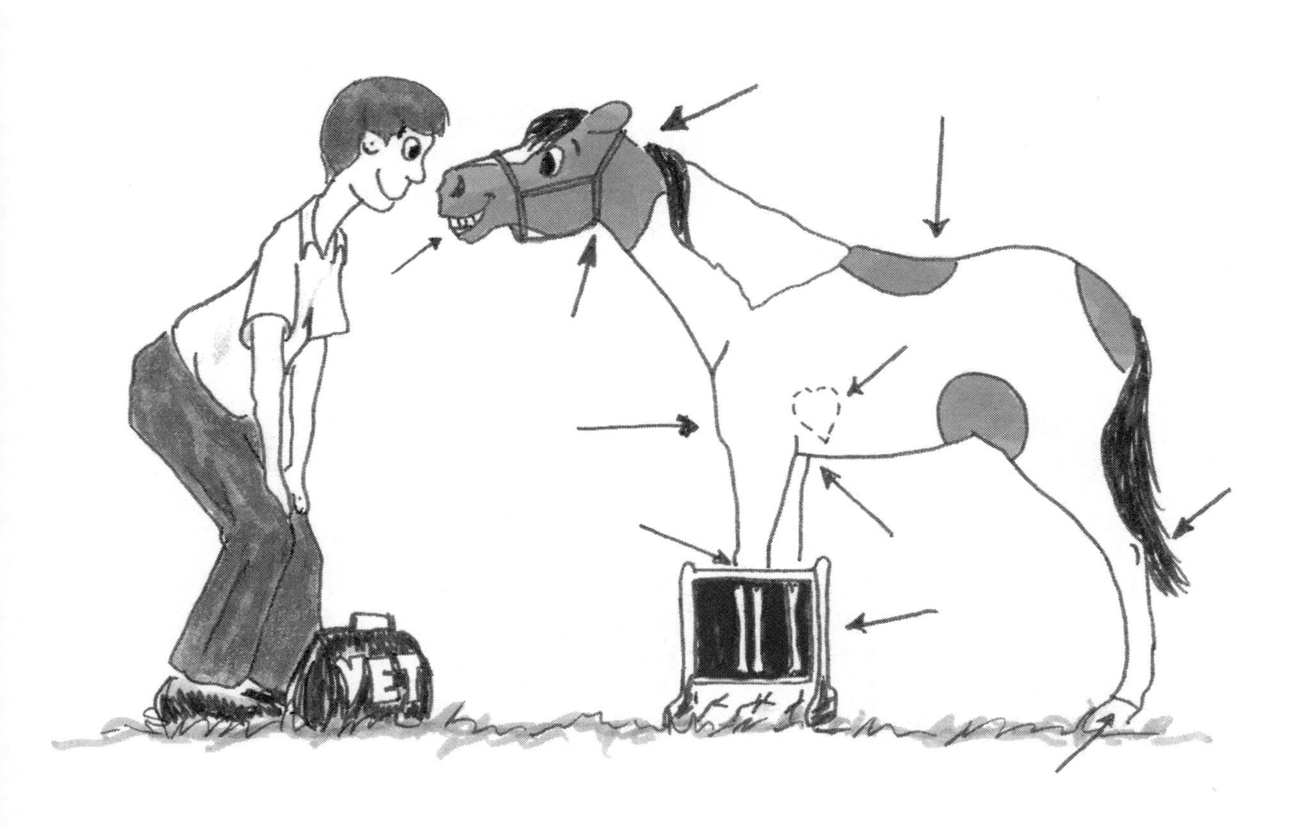

A horse doctor is called a veterinarian.

A farrier takes care of the horse's hooves and trims them to keep them healthy and balanced.

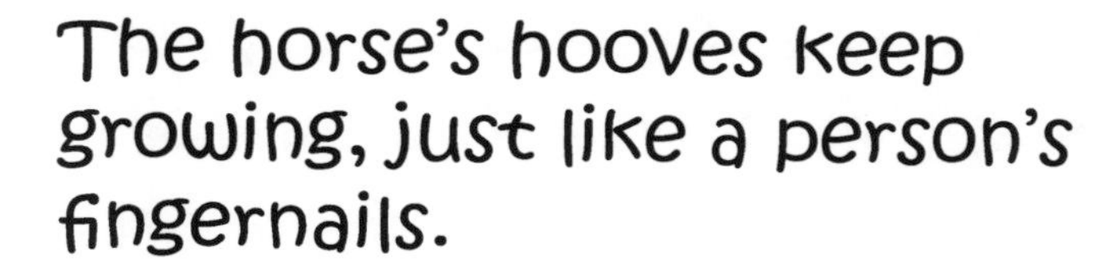

The horse's hooves keep growing, just like a person's fingernails.

Hooves that are too long, split, cracked, or very steep can make a horse lame.

A lame horse has pain in its feet and legs. A lame horse is in too much pain to be ridden.

Horses need to be groomed to keep them clean and healthy.

People use brushes and combs to groom the horse.

The rubber curry helps to clean off mud and dirt.

Body brushes clean the horse's hair and makes their coat shine.

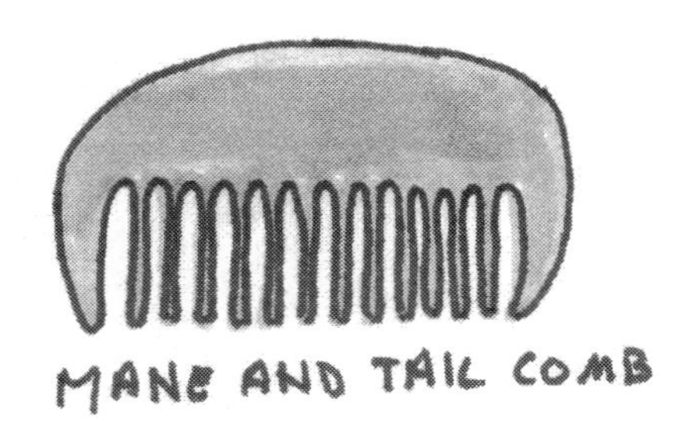

Combs untangle the mane and tail.

The hoof pick cleans dirt from the horse's hooves.

The horse needs its hooves cleaned because dirty hooves can make them get
thrush. Thrush is a hoof disease that
hurts the hooves and can make the horse
lame.

Horses have feelings and they need food, shelter, and kindness. They depend on people to take care of them.

This horse is sad because he is cold and wet. He needs shelter to protect him from the cold rain.

One of the horse's jobs is to take people for rides.

Horseback riding is fun.

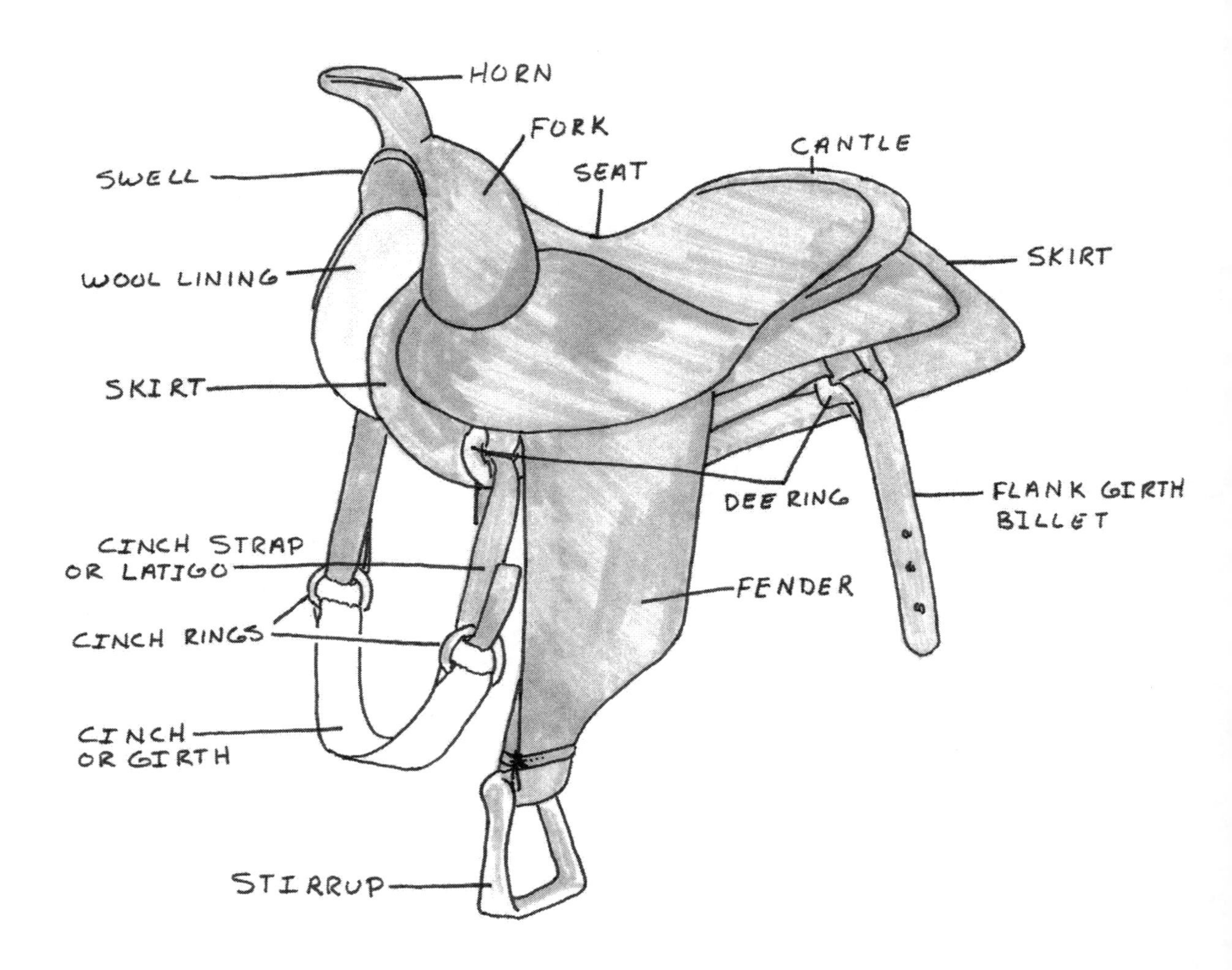

A saddle helps people to sit on the horse's back. The saddle's stirrups help a rider to balance. A rider can also hang on to the saddle if they need help to stay on.

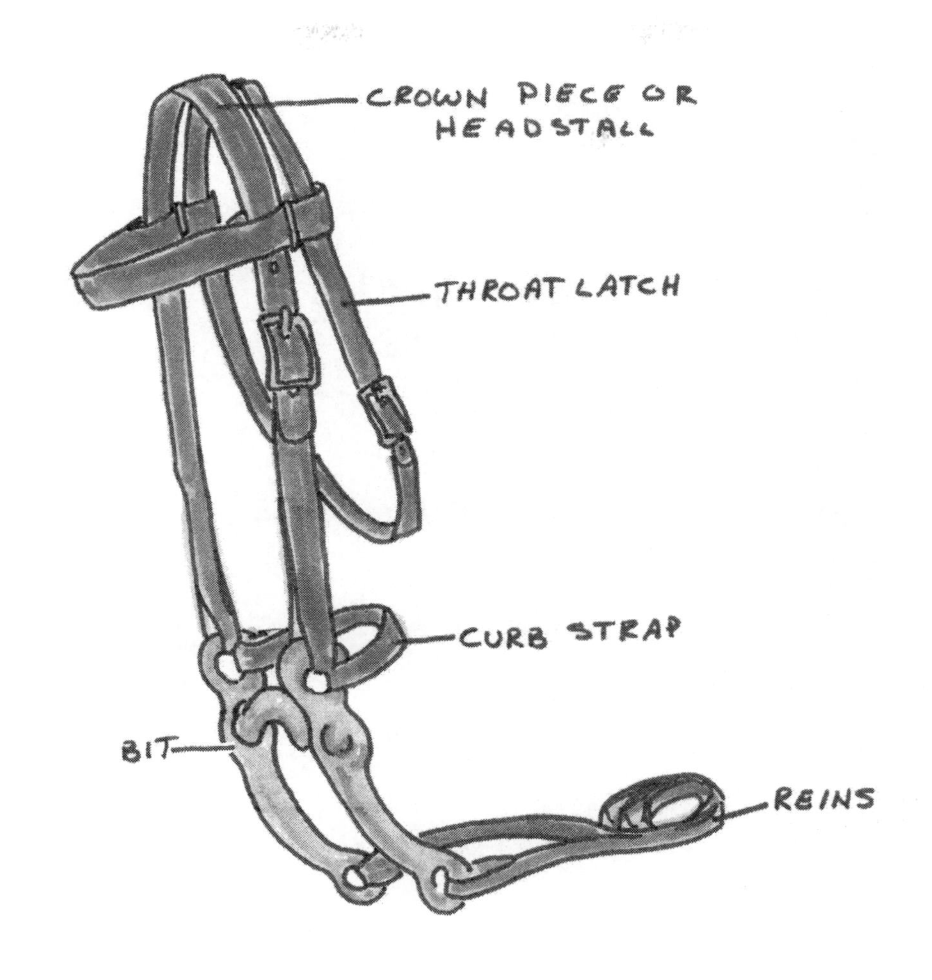

A bridle has a bit that goes into the horse's mouth. People use the bridle's reins to tell the horse what they want it to do.

The reins are attached to the bit in the horse's mouth and the rider uses them to guide the horse's head to tell it what direction to go and when to stop.

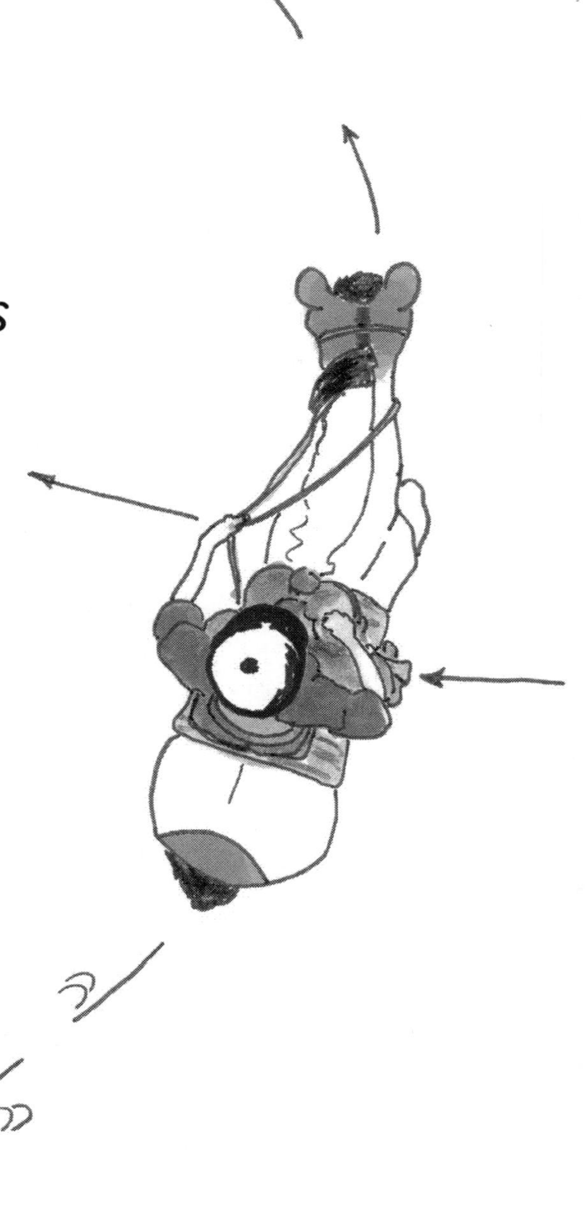

Horses do not like it when you jiggle the reins because it makes the bit bump against their teeth.

A rider always holds the reins in their hands ...

because, if a horse steps on the reins
it can hurt its mouth.

Saddles, bridles, and bits come in different sizes to fit different sized horses. The saddle and bridle should fit the horse.

If the saddle is too small or too big it could pinch the horse and hurt it's back.

The bridle fits on the horse's head and holds the bit in the horse's mouth.

If the bit is too big, it will slide through the horse's mouth and bother it. If the bit is too small, it will pinch the horse's mouth and make it sore. If the bit hangs too low, it could bump the horse's teeth.

A horse with a sore back or mouth won't want anyone to ride it.

The saddle and bridle on this horse is too big and the horse doesn't like it.

Riders need equipment too. A rider wears a helmet and boots with a heel. A helmet and boots help riders stay safe when riding a horse.

Don't ride barefoot because your foot could slip through the stirrup. Boots have a heel that stops your foot from going through the stirrup.

The helmet protects a riders head, just in case they fall.

Riders wear boots and helmets to help them stay safe around horses. Learning about horses is also an important part of being safe.

Horses are big animals and people who ride and work around them are careful to not get kicked, stepped on, or trampled.

To be safe:

Do not run up behind a horse.

Do not stand directly in front of or behind a horse.

Do not stand between the horse and a solid object or wall.

Do not make quick or sudden movements that could spook the horse.

Talk to the horse when you approach it so that it knows you are there.

Wear boots with a heel to keep your foot from slipping through the stirrup.

Wear a helmet.

Horses can be frightened by things that move quickly towards them. They can be afraid of loud noises and things they don't understand.

A frightened horse tries to run away from what it is afraid of.

A horse trainer teaches the horse how to do what the rider asks it to do. A horse trainer has a lot of experience and helps the horse to learn its job.

Some horses are just starting to learn to be ridden.

Some horses have a lot of training and know what to do.

A beginning rider should ride a well trained horse that knows what to do. A well trained horse is safer to ride and it will help the beginning rider to learn.

Horses need to be trained before they will let people ride them.

Horses use their ears to tell other horses and people how they feel.

When a horse is interested in something, it will point its ears at what it is looking at. Sometimes the horse will point its ears back at the rider because it is listening to what the rider is asking it to do.

If a horse is mad, or angry, it will pin its ears down flat on the top of its neck.

When a horse is relaxed, its ears may get floppy. Its ears will bounce a little as it moves and its body will seem a little sleepy.

Interested

Concentrating On Something Behind

Mad

Relaxed

Riders watch the horse's ears to see what kind of mood the horse is in and what they are looking at.

Horses are groomed before a saddle is put on. The hair and skin under the saddle needs to be clean so that nothing pricks the horse or hurts its back under the saddle.

The saddle is strapped onto the horse's back with a cinch. Some cinches use a buckle and some are tied to the saddle with a saddle knot.

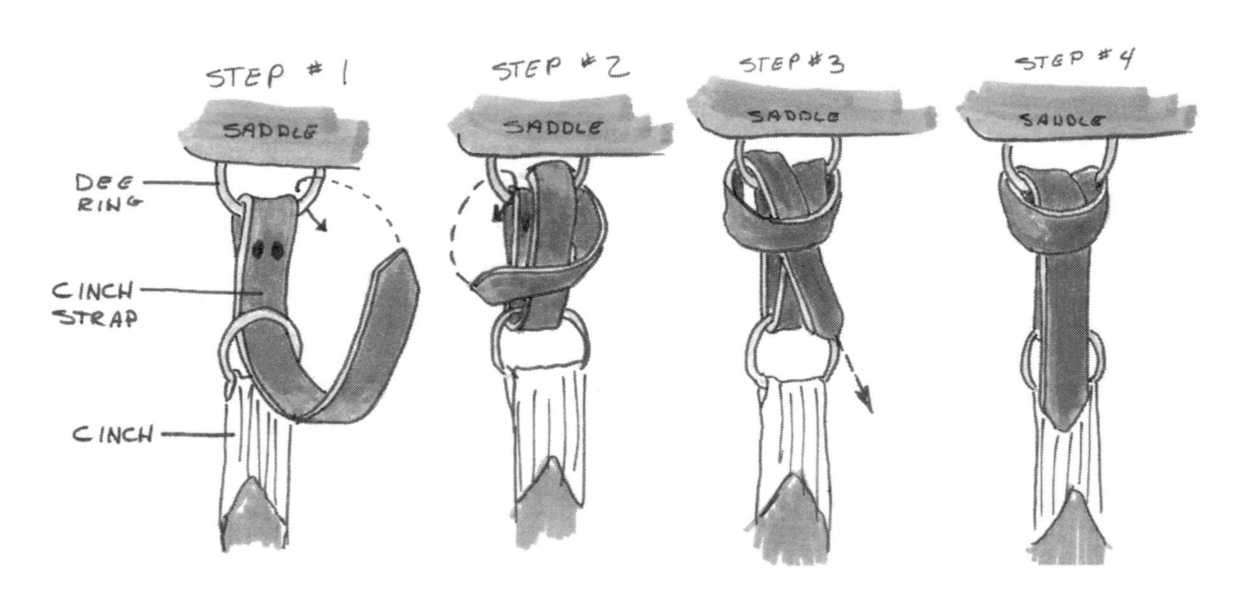

Saddle Knot

A saddle is put onto the horse's back from its left side.

Mount the horse from its left side.

To mount, put your left foot into the left stirrup and step up on the stirrup in the same way that you would walk up stairs. Don't plop down onto the horse's back, but settle gently into the saddle.

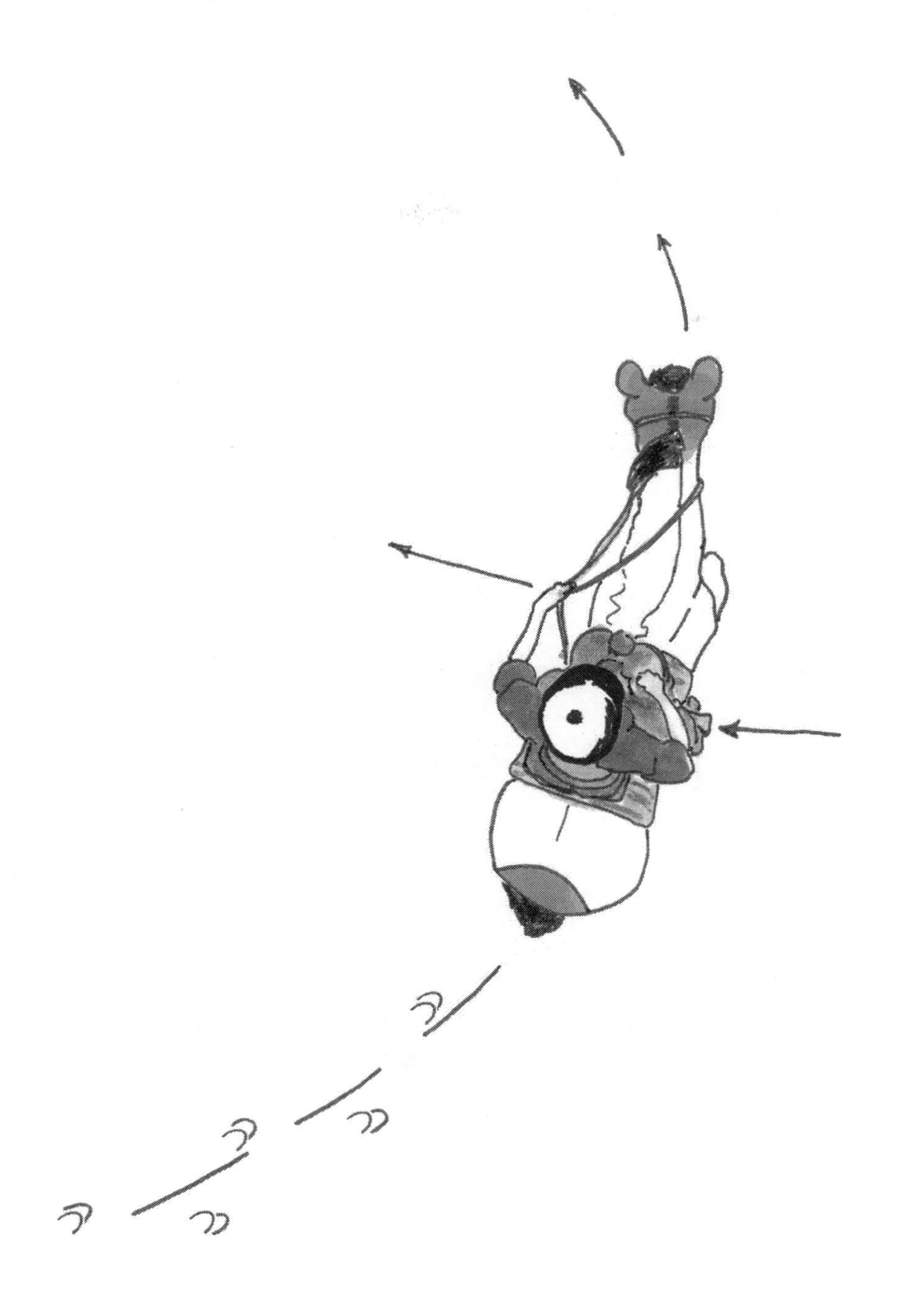

The rider points the reins in the direction they want to go and uses their leg to gently push the horse in that direction.

Horses have different gaits. A gait is how the horse uses its feet to move.

People have gaits too. People walk and they also run.

Horses walk, and trot, and canter or gallop.

The horse uses its different gaits to go at different speeds.

The walk is a slow speed.

The trot is a medium speed.

The canter or gallop is a fast speed.

If a horse tries to run away with the rider, the rider will carefully use one rein to make the horse go into a smaller and then smaller circle until it stops running.

A horse that rears stands on its hind legs and paws the air with its front legs. It may lose its balance and fall backward.

A horse that rears is not safe to ride and it needs more training from a horse trainer.

A horse that bucks will leap and jump into the air and try to throw the rider off of its back.

A horse will buck for different reasons. It may be scared, or it may be uncomfortable or hurt, or it may be confused or mad.

A horse that bucks is not safe to ride and needs more training with a horse trainer.

Sometimes, the horse does not do what you want it to.

Riders who have problems with their horses will ask a horse trainer or riding teacher for help.

The horse trainer trains the horse and helps it to understand what it is supposed to do.

The riding teacher teaches the rider how to ask the horse to do things.

If you have problems with a horse, don't get mad.

If the horse doesn't do what you want, ask for help from a horse trainer or riding teacher.

A horse has feelings and it can get tired and have sore muscles if it is worked too hard for a long time.

A rider takes care of the horse and is careful not to over work it.

A tired horse gets sweaty and hangs its head down. It will breathe hard and may stumble and trip on its feet.

A horses's job is to let people ride it.

A persons job is to take care of the horse and keep it safe.

Horseback riding can be a lot of fun when the horse and rider work together and understand each other.

Here is a basic list of stuff for horses.

Tack: horse equipment. To tack up means to put equipment on the horse

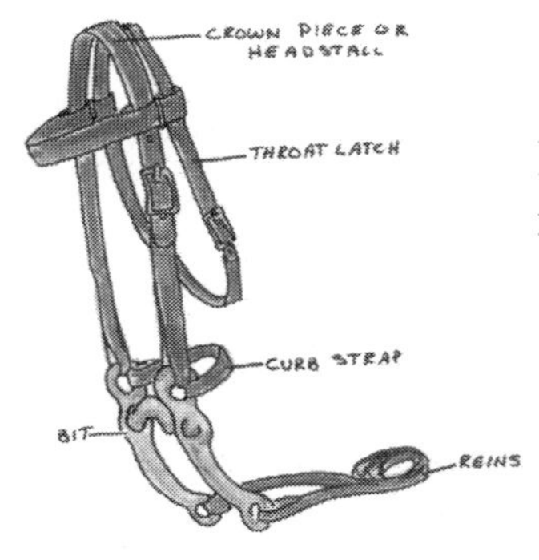

Bridle: It has a bit that goes into the horse's mouth.

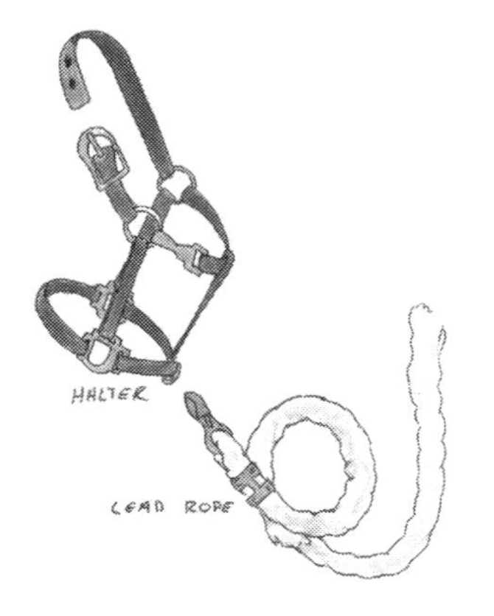

Halter: It does not have a bit.

A **panic snap** is a snap that opens when the latch is pulled down.

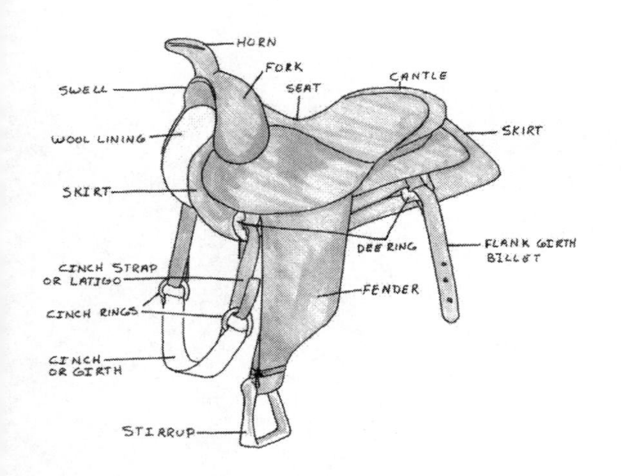

Saddle: The rider sits in the saddle on the horse's back.

Parts Of The Horse

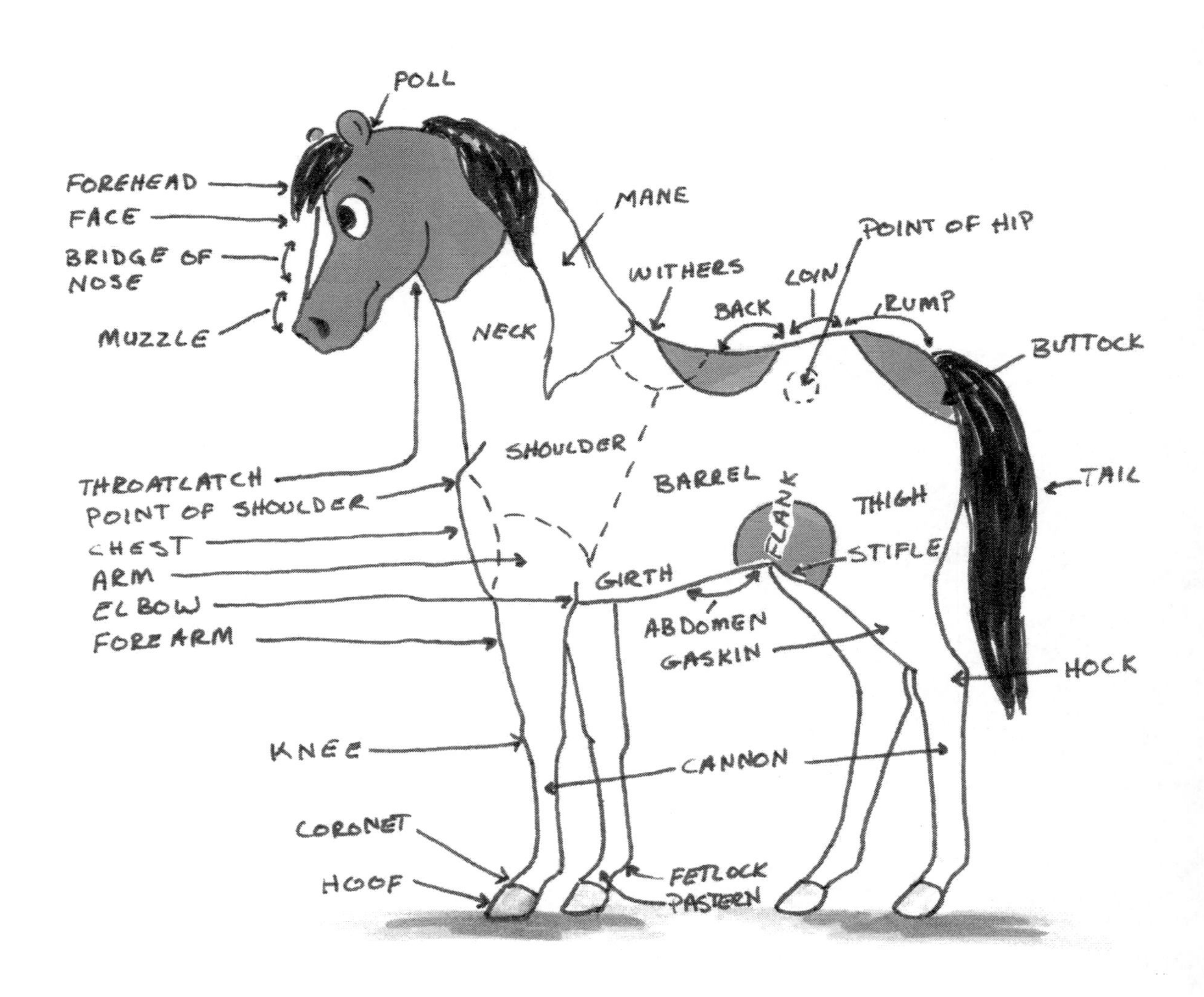

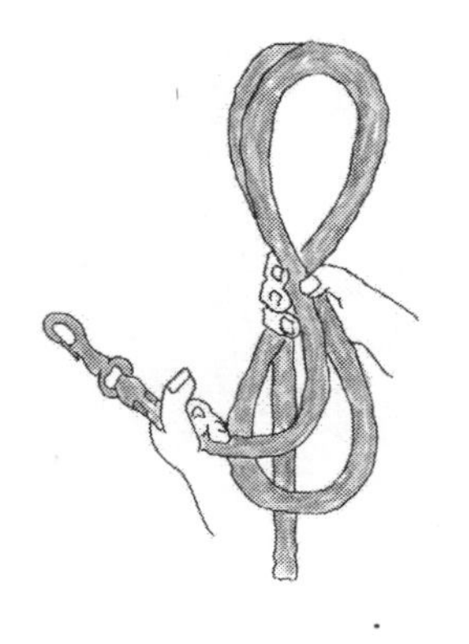

Lead rope: it snaps to the bottom ring of the halter and it is used to lead the horse.

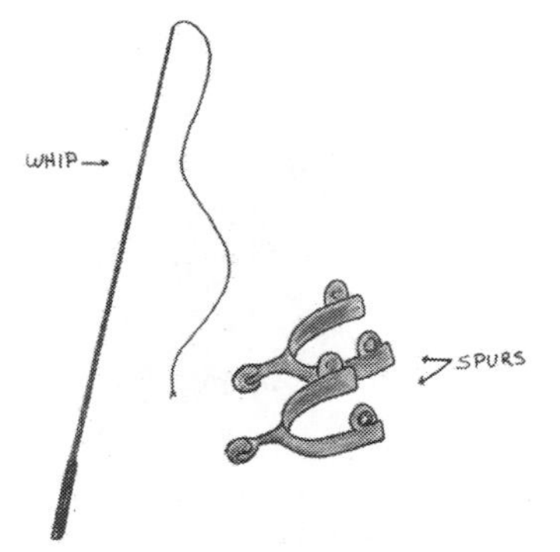

Whip and spurs: They are used to signal the horse. Beginning riders should not use spurs.

Float: To file the teeth and smooth over the sharp edges.

A horse that drops its food while eating needs its teeth floated by a veterinarian or equine dentist.

Ride safe and have fun.

Made in the USA
San Bernardino, CA
10 June 2019